WHAT'S IT REALLY LIKE TO BE A
TEACHER?

CHRISTINE HONDERS

PowerKiDS press™

New York

Published in 2020 by The Rosen Publishing Group, Inc.
29 East 21st Street, New York, NY 10010

First Edition

Editor: Greg Roza
Book Design: Michael Flynn

Photo Credits: Cover, p. 1 Jose Luis Pelaez Inc/DigitalVision/Getty Images; pp. 4, 6, 8, 10, 12, 14, 16, 18, 20, 22 (background) Apostrophe/Shutterstock.com; pp. 5, 9, 15 Monkey Business Images/Shutterstock.com; p. 7 Monashee Frantz/OJP Images/Getty Images; p. 11 skynesher/E+/Getty Images; p. 13 Satyrenko/Shutterstock.com; p. 17 Steve Debenport/E+/Getty Images; p. 19 antoniodiaz/Shutterstock.com; p. 21 stockfour/Shutterstock.com; p. 22 SS1001/Shutterstock.com.

Cataloging-in-Publication Data

Names: Honders, Christine.
Title: What's it really like to be a teacher? / Christine Honders.
Description: New York : PowerKids Press, 2020. | Series: Jobs kids want | Includes glossary and index.
Identifiers: ISBN 9781538349960 (pbk.) | ISBN 9781538349984 (library bound) | ISBN 9781538349977 (6 pack)
Subjects: LCSH: Teachers–Juvenile literature. | Teaching–Vocational guidance–Juvenile literature.
Classification: LCC LB1775.H66 2020 | DDC 371.10023–dc23
Manufactured in the United States of America

CPSIA Compliance Information: Batch #CSPK19. For Further Information contact Rosen Publishing, New York, New York at 1-800-237-9932.

CONTENTS

At the Head of the Class

You see your teacher every school day. They have lessons planned. They have fun activities for you to do. They check your homework and give you more! Teaching might look easy. But do you know what it really takes to be a teacher?

Who Are Teachers?

Teachers are the people who tell us how to do things. They explain new ideas. They give us an **education**. Teachers make sure students learn by giving them homework and tests. If you're having a problem learning something, they'll give you extra help.

Elementary School Teachers

Elementary school lasts from kindergarten to fifth grade. Elementary school teachers teach many different **subjects**, such as math, reading, writing, and science. They also teach kids good study habits. In addition, elementary school teachers show kids how to **communicate** and get along with each other.

Middle School and High School

Middle and high school teachers teach certain subjects. They also teach things like good health and **nutrition**. They push students to become more **independent**. High school teachers get kids ready for life after school. They help them get into college or learn job skills.

Teachers Outside the Classroom

Getting an education means more than just learning to read and write. Music and art teachers help us be creative. Gym teachers make our bodies stronger. **Technology** teachers teach computer skills. Some teachers teach life skills. Life skills include cooking, raising a child, and managing money.

Preschool Teachers

Preschool teachers teach kids who are three to five years old. They teach kids numbers and letters, using songs, art, and games. The kids learn to share and to work together. Preschool teachers are very important. Kids who go to preschool often do better in elementary school.

Special Education

Special education teachers work with school kids with **disabilities**. They know how to teach kids who have problems walking, talking, and learning. Special education teachers write plans that help kids with these special needs. They use special tools in the classroom.

Staying After School

Teaching can be hard work! Teachers teach a lot of information in a short time. Some kids can't keep up. Teachers often work long after the school day is over. They give extra help after school. They work nights and weekends, grading papers and making lesson plans.

Teaching the Teacher

After high school, students go to college to learn about education. Some study subjects like math or science. Students must teach in a classroom with a teacher. Then they take tests to become **certified**. After that, they have to take more college classes to stay certified.

Making the Grade

Teachers are special people. They love teaching new ideas to students. They work with kids who need help because they want everyone to do their best. If you want to make a difference in the lives of young people, become a teacher!

GLOSSARY

certified: Having the special training needed to work in a certain job.

communicate: To talk to someone else.

disability: A condition that limits what a person can do.

education: The process of receiving knowledge from others.

independent: Able to do something without help.

nutrition: The act of eating food that is needed for growth.

subject: An area of study that focuses on learning one certain topic.

technology: The use of science to solve problems.

INDEX

WEBSITES

Due to the changing nature of Internet links, PowerKids Press has developed an online list of websites related to the subject of this book. This site is updated regularly. Please use this link to access the list: www.powerkidslinks.com/JKW/teacher